THE LORD'S PRAYER

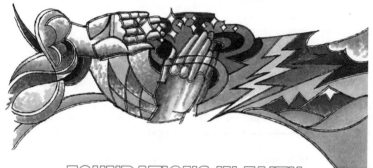

FOUNDATIONS IN FAITH
Study Guide

SAINT LOUIS

Edited by Thomas Doyle

This publication is available in braille and in large print or the visually impaired. Write to Library for the Blind, 1333 S. Kirkwood Road, St. Louis, MO 63122-7295; or call 1-800-433-3954.

CONTENTS

INTRODUCTION

The Foundations in Faith series is an introduction to the truths of God's Word as presented in Dr. Martin Luther's Small Catechism.

Why study the Catechism?

In the early Christian church, God's people confessed their faith and witnessed to the world in brief creeds. "Jesus is Lord" (1 Corinthians 12:3). "The mystery of godliness is great: He appeared in a body, was vindicated by the Spirit, was seen by angels …" (1 Timothy 3:16). These passages from New Testament, along with others, gave believers short, concise statements of faith in Jesus as Savior and Lord. In time, the church wrote and adopted new creeds to explain more fully the basics of the Christian faith.

The church also wrote and adopted catechisms as summaries of the major doctrines of Holy Scripture. At first, catechisms were tools for teachers. With the invention of the printing press, catechisms were printed for pastors, teachers of the faith, and parents to use within the congregation and at home.

Luther's Small Catechism, published in 1529, covers the "Six Chief Parts" of Christian doctrine. In Luther's words, "The Catechism is an epitome and brief transcript of the entire Holy Scripture." It is a summary and guide for believers, as they learn and reflect on the truths of God's Word.

The Foundations in Faith series explores Luther's Small Catechism in four parts: The Ten Commandments, The Apostles' Creed, The Lord's Prayer, and The Sacraments. The study guides may be used in any order (although the sequence in the Catechism is preferred), and are designed as an *introduction* or *refresher* course for congregational or personal use. Ideally, participants will learn how the Catechism presents God's Word in a clear, understandable way, in order to bring God's people to faith in Christ and to a daily life shaped and empowered by Word and Sacrament.

May God bless your study of His Word in the Catechism!

THE 1
MYSTERY
OF PRAYER

Pray Together

My God and my love,
You are mine, and I am Yours.
Deepen Your love in me, O Lord,
that I may learn how joyful it is to serve You.
Let Your love take hold of me
that I may be filled with devotion
because of Your goodness.
Then I will sing to You the song of love.
I will follow You,
and my soul will never grow tired of praising You.
In Jesus' name. Amen.

Discover

God commands and invites His people to pray. For believers, prayer is a heart to heart conversation with the heavenly Father, who shows His love in the life, death, and resurrection of His Son Jesus Christ.

Introduction

It's a simple truth: God wants His people to pray. He promises to hear and answer our prayers.

For many people, though, prayer is not simple. They ask, "What should I pray? How should I pray?" They think of prayer as a mystery.

When detectives solve mysteries, they ask fundamental questions: Who? What? When? Where? How? As we study God's Word and the Catechism, we will, as Luther notes, "value prayer as a great and precious" gift.

- What questions do you have about prayer?

- How has prayer been a part of your life in the past?

- In what ways do you want to deepen your prayer life?

Who?

God alone is God. The God revealed in the Bible is the Trinity: Father, Son, and Holy Spirit. Only prayers addressed to the triune God are acceptable to God.

God's Word

Now Daniel so distinguished himself among the administrators and the satraps by his exceptional qualities that the king planned to set him over the whole kingdom. At this, the administrators and the satraps tried to find grounds for charges against Daniel in his conduct of government affairs, but they were unable to do so. They could find no corruption in him, because he was trustworthy and neither corrupt nor negligent.

So the administrators and the satraps went as a group to the king and said: "O King Darius, live forever! The royal administrators, prefects, satraps, advisers and governors have all agreed that the king should issue an edict and enforce the decree that anyone who prays to any god or man during the next thirty days, except to you, O king, shall be thrown into the lions' den. Now, O king, issue the decree and put it in writing so that it cannot be altered—in accordance with the laws of the Medes and Persians, which cannot be repealed." So King Darius put the decree in writing.

Now when Daniel learned that the decree had been published, he went home to his upstairs room where the windows opened toward Jerusalem. Three times a day he got down on his knees and prayed, giving thanks to his God, just as he had done before. Then these men went as a group and found Daniel praying and asking God for help. (Daniel 6:3–4, 6–11)

1. In what ways do Daniel's accusers represent the temptations and pressures God's people face in the world?

2. How does Daniel demonstrate His faith in the true God?

3. How does God's love and power encourage His people in difficult, often dangerous circumstances?

Gift shops, drug stores, or supermarkets carry an assortment of greeting cards. Some of the more popular categories are "Missing You," "Friendship," and "Keep in Touch."

Imagine for a moment that God is sending you a greeting card. It shares what God wants to say to you as His child.

- What picture is on the cover?

- What words are written inside?

Through His Word, God invites us to pray. He also promises to answer our prayers. Jesus said, "I will do whatever you ask in My name, so that the Son may bring glory to the Father. You may ask Me for anything in My name, and I will do it" (John 14:13–14). In Christ, we have confidence to offer our prayers to the heavenly Father.

What?

Through His Word, God encourages us to ask for everything that we need in life. We may pray for material blessings: for health, for a steady income, for success in our work. We may pray for spiritual blessings: forgiveness, wisdom to know God's will, patience during an illness. We may offer prayers of thanks, of praise, of anguish, and of sorrow.

4. What prayers have you spoken recently?

5. What would you like to pray about in your life?

6. What would you like to pray about for your family and friends?

God's Word

Rejoice in the Lord always. I will say it again: Rejoice! Let your gentleness be evident to all. The Lord is near. Do not be anxious about anything, but in everything, by prayer and petition, with thanksgiving, present your requests to God. And the peace of God, which transcends all understanding, will guard your hearts and your minds in Christ Jesus.

Finally, brothers, whatever is true, whatever is noble, whatever is right, whatever is pure, whatever is lovely, whatever is admirable—if anything is excellent or praiseworthy—think about such things. Whatever you have learned or received or heard from me, or seen in me—put it into practice. And the God of peace will be with you. (Philippians 4:4–9)

7. What encouragement about prayer does St. Paul share with his fellow Christians?

8. How do believers know God's peace as they pray?

When?

Lloyd John Ogilvie writes about prayer:

> Prayer starts with God. It is His idea. The desire to pray is the result of God's greater desire to talk with us. He has something to say when we feel the urge to pray. He is the initiator. The keen desire to begin and end the day with prolonged prayer is His gift. The sense of need to pray for challenges and opportunities through the day is because He has wisdom and insight He wants to impart. When we face crises and suddenly feel the urge to pray for strength, that feeling is a response to the Lord's invasion of our minds, which triggers the thought of needing help, which is congealed into the desire to pray. He, not us, was the author of the longing for His help.

9. When, in your words, should Christians pray?

10. Reflect on your routines and schedule. When are you most free to spend time with God in His Word and in prayer?

Where?

God's people can pray *anywhere*! The Civil War general Thomas "Stonewall" Jackson wrote about the times and places he prayed:

> I have so fixed the habit [of prayer] in my own mind that I never raise a glass of water to my lips without lifting my heart to God in thanks and prayer for the water of life. Then, when we take our meals, there is grace. Whenever I drop a letter in the post office, I send a petition along with it for God's blessing upon its mission and the person to whom it is sent. When I break the seal of a letter just received, I stop to ask God to prepare me for its contents and make it a messenger of good. When I go to my classroom and await the arrangement of the cadets in their places, that is the time to intercede with God for them. And so in every act of the day I have made the practice of prayer habitual.

11. What situations throughout an average day prompt you to pray?

12. In what way is corporate prayer—at church, or with other believers—meaningful to you? in your family?

13. "Christians need a half hour in prayer each day, except when they are busy; then they need an hour." Agree or disagree? Share your answer.

How?

Even Jesus' disciples needed guidance in praying. "Lord, teach us to pray, just as John taught his disciples" (Luke 11:1).

How do I pray? Through His Word, God teaches us to pray

- in the name of Jesus, trusting in Him as Savior and Lord.

- with confidence, believing that in Christ God will hear our prayers and answer us.

- according to God's revealed will.

God's Word

He [Jesus] said to them, "When you pray, say:
" 'Father,
hallowed be your name,
your kingdom come.
Give us each day our daily bread.
Forgive us our sins,
for we also forgive everyone who sins against us.
And lead us not into temptation.' "

Then he said to them, "Suppose one of you has a friend, and he goes to him at midnight and says, 'Friend, lend me three loaves of bread, because a friend of mine on a journey has come to me, and I have nothing to set before him.'

"Then the one inside answers, 'Don't bother me. The door is already locked, and my children are with me in bed. I can't get up and give you anything.' I tell you, though he will not get up and give him the bread because he is his friend, yet because of the man's boldness he will get up and give him as much as he needs.

"So I say to you: Ask and it will be given to you; seek and you will find; knock and the door will be opened to you. For everyone who asks receives; he who seeks finds; and to him who knocks, the door will be opened" (Luke 11:2–10).

14. What does Jesus teach His disciples about prayer?

15. Describe a time you have "asked" in prayer like the man in the parable.

16. What comfort do you have in knowing that God *will* answer your prayers for His glory, for your good, for Jesus' sake?

God's People Pray

Faithful God, Your mercies are new to us every day.
Look on us in mercy.
Renew us by Your Holy Spirit.
Keep us safe as we work and rest.
Let Your blessing remain on us today,
and bring us to eternal life through Jesus
    Christ our Lord.
In His name, I pray. Amen.

A Verse a Day

Sunday: Be joyful always; pray continually; give thanks in all circumstances, for this is God's will for you in Christ Jesus. (1 Thessalonians 5:16–18)

Monday: May the words of my mouth and the meditation of my heart be pleasing in Your sight, O LORD, my Rock and my Redeemer. (Psalm 19:14)

Tuesday: If you remain in Me and My words remain in You, ask whatever you wish, and it will be given you. (John 15:7)

Wednesday: Give thanks to the LORD, for He is good. His love endures forever. (Psalm 136:1)

Thursday: "If you believe, you will receive whatever you ask for in prayer." (Matthew 21:22)

Friday: Before they call I will answer; while they are still speaking I will hear. (Isaiah 65:24)

Saturday: But Jesus often withdrew to lonely places and prayed. (Luke 5:16)

THE INTRODUCTION AND THE FIRST PETITION

2

Pray Together

Lord, You know what is best for me.
Give me what You will and when You will
and as much as You will.
Do with me as You know best and as it pleases You
and brings You the most honor.
Place me where You will
and guide me according to Your wisdom.
I am in Your hand as Your servant
ready to do all that You command.
In Jesus' name. Amen.

Discover

In the Lord's Prayer, God invites us to call on Him as our loving, gracious Father through Christ. Forgiven in Jesus, we grow in knowledge of His Word and live to His glory.

Introduction

A Christian poet once wrote, "The Lord's Prayer may be committed to memory quickly, but it is slowly learned by heart."

- What did the poet mean?

- When did you first hear and memorize the Lord's Prayer?

- In what ways have you "learned" the Lord's Prayer throughout your life?

The Catechism

THE INTRODUCTION
Our Father who art in heaven.

What does this mean? With these words God tenderly invites us to believe that He is our true Father and that we are His true children, so that with all boldness and confidence we may ask Him as dear children ask their dear father.

In faith, we pray "Our Father."
Martin Luther said in his devotional writings on the Lord's Prayer, "The best way to begin or introduce the prayer is to know how to address, honor, and treat the person ... how to conduct ourselves in his presence, so that he will be gracious toward us and willing to listen to us. Of all names there is none that gains us more favor with God than that of 'Father.' "

16

1. What images come to mind when you call God *Father*?

2. In general, what privileges do children enjoy from a loving father?

3. Describe how God's children may call on Him with "all boldness and confidence."

God's Word

Jesus continued: "There was a man who had two sons. The younger one said to his father, 'Father, give me my share of the estate.' So he divided his property between them.

"Not long after that, the younger son got together all he had, set off for a distant country and there squandered his wealth in wild living. After he had spent everything, there was a severe famine in that whole country, and he began to be in need. So he went and hired himself out to a citizen of that country, who sent him to his fields to feed pigs. He longed to fill his stomach with the pods that the pigs were eating, but no one gave him anything.

"When he came to his senses, he said, 'How many of my father's hired men have food to spare, and here I am starving to death! I will set out and go back to my father and say to him: Father, I have sinned against heaven and against you. I am no longer worthy to be called your son; make me like one of your hired men.' So he got up and went to his father.

"But while he was still a long way off, his father saw him and was filled with compassion for him; he ran to his son, threw his arms around him and kissed him. The son said to him, 'Father, I have sinned against heaven and against you. I am no longer worthy to be called your son.'

"But the father said to his servants, 'Quick! Bring the best robe and put it on him. Put a ring on his finger and sandals on his feet. Bring the fattened calf and kill it. Let's have a feast and celebrate. For this son of mine was dead and is alive again; he was lost and is found.' So they began to celebrate.

"Meanwhile, the older son was in the field. When he came near the house, he heard music and dancing. So he called one of the servants and asked him what was going on. 'Your brother has come,' he replied, 'and your father has killed the fattened calf because he has him back safe and sound.'

"The older brother became angry and refused to go in. So his father went out and pleaded with him. But he answered his father, 'Look! All these years I've been slaving for you and never disobeyed your orders. Yet you never gave me even a young goat so I could celebrate with my friends. But when this son of yours who has squandered your property with prostitutes comes home, you kill the fattened calf for him!'

" 'My son,' the father said, 'you are always with me, and everything I have is yours. But we had to celebrate and be glad, because this brother of yours was dead and is alive again; he was lost and is found.' " (Luke 15: 11–32)

18

4. What characteristics do you admire in the father in the parable?

5. What characteristics do the sons demonstrate by their words and actions?

6. How does the father in the parable remind you of the heavenly Father?

God Our Father

God is *our* Father. In the Introduction, we pray that God will be recognized by everyone in the world as the perfect Father: be almighty, all-powerful, all-knowing, always present for His children.

- Why did Jesus begin His prayer with *our* Father rather than *my* Father?

- What comfort do you have in knowing that you pray together with all believers, "Our Father"?

Who Art in Heaven

The phrase "who art in heaven" reminds us that God is Lord of all. God's power is not restricted to heaven or earth. His power is immeasurable.

God's Word

"The God who made the world and everything in it is the Lord of heaven and earth and does not live in temples built by hands. And He is not served by human hands, as if He needed anything, because He Himself gives all men life and breath and everything else. From one man He made every nation of men, that they should inhabit the whole earth; and He determined the times set for them and the exact places where they should live. God did this so that men would seek Him and perhaps reach out for Him and find Him, though He is not far from each one of us. 'For in Him we live and move and have our being.' As some of your own poets have said, 'We are His offspring.'

"Therefore since we are God's offspring, we should not think that the divine being is like gold or silver or stone—an image made by man's design and skill." (Acts 17:24–29)

7. How does St. Paul describe God in this speech at Mars Hill?

8. In what way is God's power intimidating to people? In what way is God's power reassuring to you?

9. The perfect relationship between the Creator and His creation was broken by the sin of Adam and Eve. But God had a plan.

a. What was God's plan to bring us back to His family?

b. How did God accomplish His plan?

10. Not only did God restore our broken relationship with Him: He made us dear children. The apostle Paul writes, "For you did not receive a spirit that makes you a slave again to fear, but you received the Spirit of sonship. And by him we cry, "Abba, Father" (Romans 8:15). What blessings have you received as a child of God through faith in Jesus?

We have the privilege of approaching God in prayer because of our faith in Christ. We are forgiven, and as forgiven children of God we can pray to Him as "our Father."

At times, however, we may not feel forgiven. We may not feel like praying. Our hearts are overwhelmed with the demands of the day. Our minds cannot fathom all the responsibilities we face at home or work. We do not know what to pray.

Good news! God has provided for our needs!

God's Word

In the same way, the Spirit helps us in our weakness. We do not know what we ought to pray for, but the Spirit Himself intercedes for us with groans that words cannot express. And He who searches our hearts knows the mind of the Spirit, because the Spirit intercedes for the saints in accordance with God's will.

And we know that in all things God works for the good of those who love Him, who have been called according to His purpose. For those God foreknew He also predestined to be conformed to the likeness of His Son, that He might be the firstborn among many brothers. And those He predestined, He also called; those He called, He also justified; those He justified, He also glorified.

What, then, shall we say in response to this? If God is for us, who can be against us? He who did not spare His own Son, but gave Him up for us all—how will He not also, along with Him, graciously give us all things? Who will bring any charge against those whom God has chosen? It is God who justifies. Who is He that condemns? Christ Jesus, who died—more than that, who was raised to life—is at the right hand of God and is also interceding for us. (Romans 8:26–34)

11. Who prays and pleads for us?

12. The Spirit "helps us in our weakness." What types of weakness do God's people face? When might our weakness discourage us from praying?

13. When the words will not come, what comfort does God's promise offer us?

The Catechism

THE FIRST PETITION
Hallowed be Thy name.

What does this mean? God's name is certainly holy in itself, but we pray in this petition that it may be kept holy among us also.

How is God's name kept holy? God's name is kept holy when the Word of God is taught in its truth and purity, and we, as the children of God, also lead holy lives according to it. Help us to do this, dear Father in heaven! But anyone who teaches or lives contrary to God's Word profanes the name of God among us. Protect us from this, heavenly Father!

To hallow God's name means to keep it holy. The name by which God revealed Himself to Moses was I AM WHO I AM, or Yahweh, which means "He is" (see Exodus 3:14–15). In Old Testament times, God's name was considered so sacred that people would not speak it or write it for fear of inadvertently misusing it. In most modern Bible translations, Yahweh is not used, but is instead translated as LORD.

God's name describes who He is and what He does. Throughout the Bible, God is described by His actions and attributes: Eternal God (Genesis 21:33); God Almighty (Genesis 17:1); Lord (Genesis 18:27); Yahweh (Exodus 3:14); Yahweh Almighty (1 Samuel 1:3); the God of Abraham, Isaac, and Jacob (Exodus 3:15); Creator (Deuteronomy 32:6).

14. How has God has impacted your life? What names would you use to describe His power and love?

15. How does worship and Bible study strengthen you as you trust and live for Christ?

God's People Pray

Heavenly Father, God of all grace,
awaken our hearts to Your Word.
We thank You for Your mercy.
We praise You for Your goodness.
Send us Your Holy Spirit,
that we hear and believe the Good News
of our salvation in Jesus Christ our Lord.
In His name, I pray. Amen.

A Verse a Day

Sunday: How great is the love the Father has lavished on us, that we should be called children of God! And that is what we are! The reason the world does not know us is that it did not know Him. (1 John 3:1)

Monday: Let us then approach the throne of grace with confidence, so that we may receive mercy and find grace to help us in our time of need. (Hebrews 4:16)

Tuesday: As a father has compassion on his children, so the Lord has compassion on those who fear Him. (Psalm 103:13)

Wednesday: You are all sons of God through faith in Christ Jesus. (Galatians 3:26)

Thursday: Our help is in the name of the Lord, the Maker of heaven and earth. (Psalm 124:8)

Friday: "You shall not misuse the name of the Lord your God, for the Lord will not hold anyone guiltless who misuses His name. (Exodus 20:7)

Saturday: Praise the Lord, O my soul; all my inmost being, praise His holy name. (Psalm 103:1)

3
SECOND AND THIRD PETITIONS

Pray Together

O Lord God, heavenly Father,
blessed be Your name now and forever.
As You will, so it is done,
and what You do is always good.
Let me, your servant, rejoice in You
and not in myself or any other thing.
You alone, O Lord, are my joy,
my hope, and my crown,
my gladness, and my honor.
In Jesus' name. Amen.

Discover

In the Lord's Prayer, God invites us to pray for the Kingdom: His blessings of forgiveness, life, and salvation in Christ. As we trust in Jesus, He leads us and strengthens us to know and live according to His Word.

Introduction

Nebuchadnezzar. Alexander. Elizabeth I. Once great monarchs, their names are seldom spoken except in history lectures. The empires they ruled are long gone, their

26

power and authority have vanished as the morning dew.

Today, too, as royal families and empires are plagued by scandal and political weakness, kingdoms are in decline. Yet one Kingdom remains strong—the kingdom of God.

- What images come to mind in the word *kingdom?*

- If you were king or queen, what type of kingdom would you want to rule?

The Catechism

THE SECOND PETITION
Thy kingdom come.

What does this mean? The kingdom of God certainly comes by itself without our prayer, but we pray in this petition that it may come to us also.

How does God's kingdom come? God's kingdom comes when our heavenly Father gives us His Holy Spirit, so that by His grace we believe His holy Word and lead godly lives here in time and there in eternity.

What is God's kingdom? God rules over His kingdom in three ways.

- God's kingdom *has come.* It is a kingdom of power: God rules over the whole universe through nature and His chosen representatives.

- God's kingdom *comes.* It is a kingdom of grace: God rules over His church on earth through the redemptive work of Jesus Christ.

- God's kingdom *will come.* It is a kingdom of glory: God rules over His church in heaven, where saints and angels praise Him forever.

"Thy kingdom come." God already rules as the eternal and exalted Maker of heaven and earth; He has established His kingdom of power.

"Thy kingdom come." Through Christ, God's people pray that the kingdoms of grace and of glory will come into our world and into our lives.

1. In what ways do you see God's rule over the universe? in history?

2. A favorite Christian hymn notes, *"He lives triumphant from the grave; He lives eternally to save; He lives exalted, throned above; He lives to rule His Church in love."* How would you describe the Lord Jesus' rule over His church?

3. What new, rich blessings do you look forward to in the kingdom of glory?

God's Word

Now the serpent was more crafty than any of the wild animals the LORD God had made. He said to the woman, "Did God really say, 'You must not eat from any tree in the garden'?"

The woman said to the serpent, "We may eat fruit from the trees in the garden, but God did say, 'You must not eat fruit from the tree that is in the middle of the garden, and you must not touch it, or you will die.'"

"You will not surely die," the serpent said to the woman.

"For God knows that when you eat of it your eyes will be opened, and you will be like God, knowing good and evil."

When the woman saw that the fruit of the tree was good for food and pleasing to the eye, and also desirable for gaining wisdom, she took some and ate it. She also gave some to her husband, who was with her, and he ate it. Then the eyes of both of them were opened, and they realized they were naked; so they sewed fig leaves together and made coverings for themselves. (Genesis 3:1–7)

4. When God created the universe, all His work was "very good" (Genesis 1:31). What happened to the good and perfect kingdom?

5. God's kingdom was opposed by evil. Who, in truth, was the serpent? How does the "old, evil foe" work in our world today?

6. How did God bring His kingdom of grace into our world?

The Kingdom of Grace

The kingdom of grace has come in Christ. Through His life, death, and resurrection Christ has broken the power of sin, death, and Satan. He has reconciled us to the heavenly Father, taking away our guilt and shame. Through faith in Jesus we belong to God's kingdom of grace. The Holy Spirit keeps us in faith and brings us to the kingdom of glory—life eternal with Christ.

How does God's kingdom of grace come to us?

When we are baptized, the heavenly Father gives us the Holy Spirit, who works faith in our hearts.

By God's grace, we trust in Christ for our salvation.

By Christ's strength, we believe God's Word and live as His forgiven, renewed people.

- How did the heavenly Father bring you into His kingdom of grace?

- What comfort and encouragement do you have in knowing that Christ lives in you and guides and strengthens you through His Word?

The Catechism

THE THIRD PETITION

Thy will be done on earth as it is in heaven.

What does this mean? The good and gracious will of God is done even without our prayer, but we pray in this petition that it may be done among us also.

How is God's will done? God's will is done when He breaks and hinders every evil plan and purpose of the devil, the world, and our sinful nature, which do not want us to hallow God's name or let His kingdom come;

and when He strengthens and keeps us firm in His Word and faith until we die.

This is His good and gracious will.

What is God's will? How can I know God's will for my life?

The Lord's Prayer presents the answer: God desires that His name be kept holy and that His kingdom come. By praying "Thy will be done," God's people are asking the heavenly Father to fulfill His promise to save because of Christ.

7. In what ways have you seen God "break and hinder" evil in our world?

8. In what ways are God's people vulnerable when we rely on our strength and resources?

9. "The center of God's will is our only safety" (Betsie Ten Boom). What comfort do you have in knowing "the center" is in Christ?

The Heavenly Father's Will

In *Armed and Dangerous* (St. Louis: Concordia, 1997) Jane Fryar writes, our heavenly Father wants us

to bring our every need and concern to Him. He gave His only Son into death for us. He *wants* the best for us, and He *will do* the very best things for us and for those whom we bring to Him in prayer …

We need not drown in doubt. We need not struggle to remake ourselves into the image of some kind of spiritual supermen or wonder-women. We need not grope around in the murky waters of our circumstances trying to find our own spiritual bootstraps so that we can yank ourselves out of the swamp and away from the jaws of the alligators. Instead, we can call out to Christ. We can confess our weakness and ask for His strength. We can keep looking to His Word of truth. We can trust Him to work through that Word even when, at the time, it seems dry as sawdust.

- What joy do you have in knowing God wants the best for your life?

God's Word

Then Jesus told them many things in parables, saying: "A farmer went out to sow his seed. As he was scattering the seed, some fell along the path, and the birds came and ate it up. Some fell on rocky places, where it did not have much soil. It sprang up quickly, because the soil was shallow. But when the sun came up, the plants were scorched, and they withered because they had no root. Other seed fell among thorns, which grew up and choked the plants. Still other seed fell on good soil, where it produced a crop—a hundred, sixty or thirty times what was sown. He who has ears, let him hear." ...

"Listen then to what the parable of the sower means: When anyone hears the message about the kingdom and does not understand it, the evil one comes and snatches away what was sown in his heart. This is the seed sown along the path. The one who received the seed that fell on rocky places is the man who hears the word and at once receives it with joy. But since he has no root, he lasts only a short time. When trouble or persecution comes because of the word, he quickly falls away. The one who received the seed that fell among the thorns is the man who hears the word, but the worries of this life and the deceitfulness of wealth choke it, making it unfruitful. But the one who received the seed that fell on good soil is the man who hears the word and understands it. He produces a crop, yielding a hundred, sixty or thirty times what was sown." (Matthew 13:3–9, 18–23)

10. In what ways does the seed represent the Word of God?

11. In what ways do the soils represent our experiences today?

12. How does the parable show that God's kingdom comes and God's will is done through His Word?

God's People Pray

Almighty Father, send us Your Holy Spirit.
Fill us with the wisdom from above.
Let Your Word take root in our lives,
and be preached throughout the whole world.
Let Your people know the joy of faith in Christ.
Keep us strong in faith, that we may serve You
all the days of our life.
Through Jesus Christ, our Lord. Amen.

A Verse a Day

Sunday: The LORD has established His throne in heaven, and His kingdom rules over all. (Psalm 103:19)

Monday: Jesus answered, "I tell you the truth, no one can enter the kingdom of God unless he is born of water and the Spirit. (John 3:5)

Tuesday: The Lord will rescue me from every evil attack and will bring me safely to His heavenly kingdom. To Him be glory for ever and ever. Amen. (2 Timothy 4:18)

Wednesday: Ask the Lord of the harvest, therefore, to send out workers into His harvest field. (Matthew 9:38)

Thursday: "For my Father's will is that everyone who looks to the Son and believes in Him shall have eternal life, and I will raise Him up at the last day." (John 6:40)

Friday: [God] wants all men to be saved and to come to a knowledge of the truth. (1 Timothy 2:4)

Saturday: That is why I am suffering as I am. Yet I am not ashamed, because I know whom I have believed, and am convinced that He is able to guard what I have entrusted to Him for that day. (2 Timothy 1:12)

THE 4 FOURTH PETITION

Pray Together

O Lord, my God,
You are all my riches,
and everything I have is from You.
You alone are good, just, and holy.
You put all things in order,
You give all things,
and fill all things with Your goodness.
Remember Your mercies, Lord,
and fill my heart with Your grace.
In Jesus' name. Amen.

Discover

In the Lord's Prayer, God invites us to pray for all our needs. Because of His mercy in Christ, our Father provides for us, body and soul, and blesses us with His love.

Introduction

"When the heart is full, the lips are silent."

It's easy, in times of prosperity, to take God's blessings for granted. The abundance we see and experience all around us too often leads to "an attitude of ingratitude."

- How do we take for granted the material blessings of our world?

- Why does prosperity sometimes lead to self-satisfaction?

The Catechism

THE FOURTH PETITION
Give us this day our daily bread.

What does this mean? God certainly gives daily bread to everyone without our prayers, even to all evil people, but we pray in this petition that God would lead us to realize this and to receive our daily bread with thanksgiving.

What is meant by daily bread? Daily bread includes everything that has to do with the support and needs of the body, such as food, drink, clothing, shoes, house, home, land, animals, money, goods, a devout husband or wife, devout children, devout workers, devout and faithful rulers, good government, good weather, peace, health, self-control, good reputation, good friends, faithful neighbors, and the like.

In his book *Great Prayers* (St. Louis: Concordia, 1968) Harry Huxhold has written of the Lord's Prayer: "The first three petitions center in the person of God. The fourth petition governs all that we need for our earthly existence. The last three petitions cover all our spiritual needs for the past, present, and future."

When we pray, "Give us this day our daily bread," we acknowledge our dependence on God for everything that supports our life.

1. How does Luther's explanation of "daily bread" describe our many needs? What other needs would you add?

2. Describe the various ways God *gives* us daily bread.

3. How do you show thankfulness for the "little blessings" of God in your life?

God's Word

Now Elijah the Tishbite, from Tishbe in Gilead, said to Ahab, "As the LORD, the God of Israel, lives, whom I serve, there will be neither dew nor rain in the next few years except at my word."

Then the word of the LORD came to Elijah: "Leave here, turn eastward and hide in the Kerith Ravine, east of the Jordan. You will drink from the brook, and I have ordered the ravens to feed you there."

So he did what the LORD had told him. He went to the Kerith Ravine, east of the Jordan, and stayed there. The ravens brought him bread and meat in the morning and bread and meat in the evening, and he drank from the brook.

Some time later the brook dried up because there had been no rain in the land. Then the word of the LORD came to him: "Go at once to Zarephath of Sidon and stay there. I have commanded a widow in that place to supply you with food." So he went to Zarephath. When he came to the town gate, a widow was there gathering sticks. He called to her and asked, "Would you bring me a little water in a jar so I may have a drink?" As she was going to get it, he called, "And bring me, please, a piece of bread."

"As surely as the LORD your God lives," she replied, "I don't have any bread—only a handful of flour in a jar and a little oil in a jug. I am gathering a few sticks to take home and make a meal for myself and my son, that we may eat it—and die."

Elijah said to her, "Don't be afraid. Go home and do as you have said. But first make a small cake of bread for me from what you have and bring it to me, and then make something for yourself and your son. For this is what the LORD, the God of Israel, says: 'The jar of flour will not be used up and the jug of oil will not run dry until the day the LORD gives rain on the land.' "

She went away and did as Elijah had told her. So there was food every day for Elijah and for the woman and her family. For the jar of flour was not used up and the jug of oil did not run dry, in keeping with the word of the LORD spoken by Elijah. (1 Kings 17:1–16).

4. hich words describe Elijah's situation? the widow's situation?

5. How did God provide for Elijah? for the widow?

6. What does the story reveal about God's concern and provision for His people?

Daily Bread

God invites us to pray for our daily bread. As we regularly pray for our physical needs, we recognize that our entire life depends on God: nothing happens apart from His fatherly, divine goodness and mercy. In faith, we look to God for all blessings, and we receive His gifts with thankful hearts and lives.

- Respond to the statement, "I work hard for everything I have! Why should I be thankful?"

- How does knowing God as the gracious Giver encourage you to share His gifts with others?

This Day

"Each day has trouble of its own" (Matthew 6:34).

Jesus' words are as timely today as they were 2,000 years ago. Clothes for the children. Transportation. Job security. The list goes on and on. Anxiety over life is a universal experience.

7. What urgent needs and concerns are you facing *today?*

8. How has God provided for you *today*?

9. What assurance do you have from God's Word about the future?

God's Word

"Therefore I tell you, do not worry about your life, what you will eat or drink; or about your body, what you will wear. Is not life more important than food, and the body more important than clothes? Look at the birds of the air; they do not sow or reap or store away in barns, and yet your heavenly Father feeds them. Are you not much more valuable than they? Who of you by worrying can add a single hour to his life?

"And why do you worry about clothes? See how the lilies of the field grow. They do not labor or spin. Yet I tell you that not even Solomon in all his splendor was dressed like one of these. If that is how God clothes the grass of the field, which is here today and tomorrow is thrown into the fire, will he not much more clothe you, O you of little faith?

So do not worry, saying, 'What shall we eat?' or 'What shall we drink?' or 'What shall we wear?' For the pagans run after all these things, and your heavenly Father knows that you need them. But seek first His kingdom and His righteousness, and all these things will be given to you as well. Therefore do not worry about tomorrow, for tomorrow will worry about itself. Each day has enough trouble of its own. (Matthew 6:25–34)

10. What does Jesus mean, "Life is more important than food ... the body more important than clothes?"

11. In what ways do we doubt God's goodness and provision by worrying?

12. What does Jesus reveal about God's goodness in the words, "all these things will be given to you as well"?

God's People Pray

Thank You, heavenly Father, for all Your
gifts.
We praise You for Your creation, Your daily
goodness,
and for all the blessings of this life.
We praise You for our salvation in Christ.
Give us thankful hearts,
that we may live to Your praise.
Help us to walk before You in holiness
all the days of our life.
Receive us into Your heavenly Kingdom,
through Your rich mercy in Christ.
In His name, I pray. Amen.

A Verse a Day

Sunday: The eyes of all look to You, and You give them their food at the proper time. You open Your hand and satisfy the desires of every living thing. (Psalm 145:15–16)

Monday: 'For in Him we live and move and have our being.' As some of your own poets have said, 'We are His offspring.' (Acts 17:28)

Tuesday; Praise the LORD. Give thanks to the LORD, for He is good; His love endures forever. (Psalm 106:1)

Wednesday: Speak to one another with psalms, hymns and spiritual songs. Sing and make music in your heart to the Lord, always giving thanks to God the Father for everything, in the name of our Lord Jesus Christ. (Ephesians 5:19–20)

Thursday: He will call upon me, and I will answer him; I will be with him in trouble, I will deliver him and honor him. (Psalm 91:15)

Friday: And do not forget to do good and to share with others, for with such sacrifices God is pleased. (Hebrews 13:16)

Saturday: Cast all your anxiety on Him because He cares for you. (1 Peter 5:7)

THE 5
FIFTH
PETITION

Pray Together

O Lord of love,
You know my many weaknesses and needs,
the many sins that afflict me,
and how often I am discouraged, tempted,
troubled, and defiled.
I come to You for healing,
and I pray for Your strength.
Lord, You know all things,
to You my inward thoughts are open.
You alone can perfectly guide and help me.
In Jesus' name. Amen.

Discover

In the Lord's Prayer, God invites us to ask for His rich mercy. Because of Christ, our heavenly Father forgives our sins and strengthens us to forgive our fellow sinners.

Introduction

"In Lake Wobegon," Garrison Keillor remarks, "we don't forget mistakes."

Should we forgive and forget? Most people would nod their head "yes"—*in theory*. Real life is often a different story.

- Why is it difficult to forgive and forget *in real life*?

- What would life be like without forgiveness?

The Catechism

THE FIFTH PETITION

And forgive us our trespasses as we forgive those who trespass against us.

What does this mean? We pray in this petition that our Father in heaven would not look at our sins, or deny our prayer because of them. We are neither worthy of the things for which we pray, nor have we deserved them, but we ask that He would give them all to us by grace, for we daily sin much and surely deserve nothing but punishment. So we too will sincerely forgive and gladly do good to those who sin against us.

The last three petitions of the Lord's Prayer deal with matters of the heart: God's heart toward us.

"Forgive us our trespasses." By praying these words, we confess we are sinners. We sin every day and always stand in need of forgiveness. We ask the heavenly Father to forgive our sins through His mercy in Jesus Christ our Lord.

1. Which words from the Explanation describe our natural, sinful condition?

2. How does sin affect our daily life? our relationships? our communities?

3. In what way does God "look beyond" our sin to see perfect goodness?

God's Word

In the year that King Uzziah died, I saw the Lord seated on a throne, high and exalted, and the train of His robe filled the temple. Above Him were seraphs, each with six wings: With two wings they covered their faces, with two they covered their feet, and with two they were flying. And they were calling to one another:

"Holy, holy, holy is the LORD Almighty;
the whole earth is full of His glory."

At the sound of their voices the doorposts and thresholds shook and the temple was filled with smoke.

"Woe to me!" I cried. "I am ruined! For I am a man of unclean lips, and I live among a people of unclean lips, and my eyes have seen the King, the LORD Almighty."

Then one of the seraphs flew to me with a live coal

in his hand, which he had taken with tongs from the altar. With it he touched my mouth and said, "See, this has touched your lips; your guilt is taken away and your sin atoned for."

Then I heard the voice of the Lord saying, "Whom shall I send? And who will go for us?" And I said, "Here am I. Send me!" (Isaiah 6:1–8)

4. Describe the prophet Isaiah's response to the holy, majestic God.

5. What does God, through the seraph (angel), do for Isaiah?

6. What is Isaiah's response to the goodness and mercy of God?

Grace Lake

How can we picture God's grace? In *Living the Lord's Prayer* (St. Louis: Concordia, 1994), Richard Andersen notes,

Grace is like that vast lake in the mountains, crystal clear, shimmering in the golden sunshine, and as pure as melted snow can be, unadulterated and uncontaminated. Grace Lake, however, is oceanic in size; it is unlimited, for no drought can empty it, nor can any thirst dry it up …

This vast sea of grace came into being, because Jesus, lifted upon the towering cross of Calvary, lovingly gave His life for you and me and everyone everywhere for all time. … It is not a hidden sea, this ocean of forgiveness. We know where it is and how to receive its life-giving waters. All we need do is ask for it; and, in Christ's name and because of Jesus' triumph, it is ours.

- How is Christ's forgiveness toward you like an "oceanic lake"?

- How can you point others to the limitless forgiveness of Christ?

"As We Forgive Those Who Trespass Against Us"

A sign on the property line warns "No Trespassing." A trespass is a "step across." We walk across the boundary. We go where we should not go.

At root, sin is trespass. We step across the boundaries God has established. We go where God has forbidden us to go. Ultimately, all sin is a trespass against God. But sin also affects people around us.

7. Think about a time when you have forgiven some-one. Was it easy or difficult to forgive? If possible, share your answer.

8. Think about a time when someone forgave you. Was it easy or difficult to accept forgiveness? If possible, share your answer.

9. How has Christ's forgiveness restored broken relationships in your life?

God's Word

When Joseph's brothers saw that their father was dead, they said, "What if Joseph holds a grudge against us and pays us back for all the wrongs we did to him?" So they sent word to Joseph, saying, "Your father left these instructions before he died: 'This is what you are to say to Joseph: I ask you to forgive your brothers the sins and the wrongs they committed in treating you so badly.' Now please forgive the sins of the servants of the God of your father." When their message came to him, Joseph wept.

His brothers then came and threw themselves down before him. "We are your slaves," they said.

But Joseph said to them, "Don't be afraid. Am I in the place of God? You intended to harm me, but God intended it for good to accomplish what is now being done, the saving of many lives. So then, don't be afraid. I will provide for you and your children." And he reassured them and spoke kindly to them. (Genesis 50:15–21)

10. What was Joseph's attitude toward the hurt his brothers inflicted on him?

11. What was Joseph's attitude toward his brothers?

12. In what way is Joseph a "picture" of Jesus and His attitude toward us?

God wants—and invites—us to forgive one another through the grace and strength of Christ. By the power of the Holy Spirit, a forgiven heart forgives. When we forgive others, we show in our lives that we *truly* believe God has forgiven us.

In the Large Catechism Martin Luther writes, "For just as God in His grace forgives everything by which we sin much against Him every day, so we also must constantly forgive our neighbor who does us harm, violence, and injustice, treats us with abominably shabby tricks, and the like. If you do not forgive, do not imagine that God will forgive you. ... But you are forgiven not on account of the forgiveness you granted to your neighbor, for God forgives completely and for nothing, out of pure grace and because He promised it."

God's Word

Then Peter came to Jesus and asked, "Lord, how many times shall I forgive my brother when he sins against me? Up to seven times?"

Jesus answered, "I tell you, not seven times, but seventy-seven times.

"Therefore, the kingdom of heaven is like a king who wanted to settle accounts with his servants. As he began the settlement, a man who owed him ten thousand talents was brought to him. Since he was not able to pay, the master ordered that he and his wife and his children and all that he had be sold to repay the debt.

"The servant fell on his knees before him. 'Be patient with me,' he begged, 'and I will pay back everything.' The servant's master took pity on him, canceled the debt and let him go.

"But when that servant went out, he found one of his fellow servants who owed him a hundred denarii. He grabbed him and began to choke him. 'Pay back what you owe me!' he demanded.

"His fellow servant fell to his knees and begged him, 'Be patient with me, and I will pay you back.'

"But he refused. Instead, he went off and had the man thrown into prison until he could pay the debt. When the other servants saw what had happened, they were greatly distressed and went and told their master everything that had happened.

"Then the master called the servant in. 'You wicked servant,' he said, 'I canceled all that debt of yours because you begged me to. Shouldn't you have had mercy on your fellow servant just as I had on you?' In anger his master turned him over to the jailers to be tortured, until he should pay back all he owed.

"This is how My heavenly Father will treat each of

you unless you forgive your brother from your heart."
(Matthew 18:21–35)

13. How does the wicked servant demonstrate an *unforgiven* and *unforgiving* heart?

14. Is the king justified in punishing the wicked servant? Why or why not?

15. How does Christ's limitless love and forgiveness toward you strengthen you to live in love and forgiveness toward others?

God's People Pray

Almighty God,
Give us Your grace in Christ.
Help us to cast off the works of darkness.
Make us stand firm with the armor of light.
Forgive our sins.
Strengthen our faith.
Lead us to live in peace with one another.
Prepare us for the Last Day,
when we will rise to eternal life
through our Lord Jesus Christ.
In His name, I pray. Amen.

A Verse a Day

Sunday: He who conceals his sins does not prosper, but whoever confesses and renounces them finds mercy. (Proverbs 28:13)

Monday: 'For the director of music. A psalm of David. When the prophet Nathan came to him after David had committed adultery with Bathsheba.' Have mercy on me, O God, according to Your unfailing love; according to Your great compassion blot out my transgressions. Wash away all my iniquity and cleanse me from my sin. (Psalm 51:1–2)

Tuesday: Then I acknowledged my sin to You and did not cover up my iniquity. I said, "I will confess my transgressions to the LORD"—and You forgave the guilt of my sin. Selah (Psalm 32:5)

Wednesday: Be kind and compassionate to one another, forgiving each other, just as in Christ God forgave you. (Ephesians 4:32)

Thursday: If You, O LORD, kept a record of sins, O Lord, who could stand? But with You there is forgiveness; therefore You are feared. (Psalm 130:3–4)

Friday: Let the peace of Christ rule in your hearts, since as members of one body you were called to peace. And be thankful. (Colossians 3:15)

Saturday: But God demonstrates His own love for us in this: While we were still sinners, Christ died for us. (Romans 5:8)

THE SIXTH AND SEVENTH PETITIONS AND THE CONCLUSION

6

Pray Together

Most kind Lord Jesus,
grant me Your grace.
Let it be always with me and work in me
and preserve me to the end.
Grant that I may always desire and will
whatever is most pleasing and acceptable
to You.
Let Your will be mine,
and let my will always follow Yours and
conform to it.
Grant me above all else,
to find in You perfect peace and rest
for my body and soul.
In Jesus' name. Amen.

Discover

In the Lord's Prayer, God invites us to ask Him for power and protection against all danger. As our loving Father in Christ, God guides us and keeps us safe as we serve Him throughout our life.

Introduction

Oscar Wilde wrote, "I can resist everything except temptation."

In many respects, modern life welcomes temptations. From "harmless" pleasures to dangerous adventures, the message is the same: Don't resist! Give in!

- From your experience, how do people generally view temptation?

- "No Fear." Why is the phrase a deceptive—even dangerous—slogan for life?

The Catechism

THE SIXTH PETITION
And lead us not into temptation.

What does this mean? God tempts no one. We pray in this petition that God would guard and keep us so that the devil, the world, and our sinful nature may not deceive us or mislead us into false belief, despair, and other great shame and vice. Although we are attacked by these things, we pray that we may finally overcome them and win the victory.

The Scriptures use the word *temptation* in two ways:
- The testing of our faith, which God allows and uses to bring us closer to Him.
- The efforts of our enemies to entice us from Christ and faith and to bring us to despair and spiritual ruin.

In the Lord's Prayer, we pray that God will not let us "fall and yield to trials and temptations."

1. Which three enemies deceive God's people and lead us toward doubt and sin?

2. What temptations do we face today at home? at work? in our communities and nation?

3. How do God's people "overcome" temptation and "win the victory?"

God's Word

Then Jesus was led by the Spirit into the desert to be tempted by the devil. After fasting forty days and forty nights, He was hungry. The tempter came to Him and said, "If You are the Son of God, tell these stones to become bread."

Jesus answered, "It is written: 'Man does not live on bread alone, but on every word that comes from the mouth of God.'"

Then the devil took Him to the holy city and had Him stand on the highest point of the temple. "If You are the Son of God," he said, "throw Yourself down. For it is written:

" 'He will command His angels concerning you, and they will lift you up in their hands, so that you will not strike your foot against a stone.'"

Jesus answered him, "It is also written: 'Do not put the Lord your God to the test.'"

Again, the devil took Him to a very high mountain and showed Him all the kingdoms of the world and their splendor. "All this I will give You," he said, "if you will bow down and worship me."

Jesus said to Him, "Away from me, Satan! For it is written: 'Worship the Lord your God, and serve Him only.'"

Then the devil left Him, and angels came and attended Him. (Matthew 4:1–11)

4. In what ways do Jesus' temptations reflect the kinds of temptations we face today?

5. How does Jesus answer the devil? In what way are His responses a model for believers?

6. How does God's Word strengthen you to resist Satan's temptations?

Leading Us Not into Temptation

Martin Luther writes, *"Leading us not into temptation* consists of God giving us the power and strength to resist it even though the tribulation itself is not turned aside nor put to an end. For not one of us can successfully bypass temptation and enticements as long as we are living in the flesh and the devil is lurking about. Nothing else is to be expected than that we shall suffer trials and temptations, yes, even find ourselves bogged in them. However, what we pray for here is that we may not fall down into them and be drowned" (Large Catechism).

In Christ, God's people stand firm in faith together!

- To whom do you turn for support and encouragement in temptation?

- How can your congregation and fellow believers help others in their temptations?

The Catechism

THE SEVENTH PETITION
But deliver us from evil.

What does this mean? We pray in this petition, in summary, that our Father in heaven would rescue us from every evil of body and soul, possessions and reputation, and finally, when our last hour comes, give us a blessed end, and graciously take us from this valley of sorrow to Himself in heaven.

Richard Andersen, in *Living the Lord's Prayer,* (St. Louis: Concordia, 1994), offers a striking portrait of "The Tempests of Life."

Satan is his name; temptation is his game. His intention is so to engage us in the terror of a tempest that we deny the very One who quiets swirling seas and storm-force winds with the word "peace."

Our journey in life is not always a peace drive along shaded lanes with a cloudless sky and a bright sun. We're often caught in emotional gusty squalls or spiritual drenching downpours. Life is not free of storms; blizzard conditions seem to immobilize us. Yet we can have sunshine in the soul.

Here is certainty on which to depend regardless of the gale force winds and the deluge. In Christ the storm is stilled.

7. What types of evils are prevalent today? In what ways is evil like a tempest in our world?

8. How has God rescued us from the greatest evil?

9. In what ways does the heavenly Father *rescue* you from daily evils and keep you in His love and care?

Our world *is* spoiled by sin. Life *is* often filled with hardship and sorrow. Yet in Christ God will keep us from harm or bring us safely through harm to His eternal kingdom.

God's Word

When it was decided that we would sail for Italy, Paul and some other prisoners were handed over to a centurion named Julius, who belonged to the Imperial Regiment. We boarded a ship and … put out to sea. …

58

Before very long, a wind of hurricane force, called the "northeaster," swept down from the island. The ship was caught by the storm and could not head into the wind; so we gave way to it and were driven along. … We took such a violent battering from the storm that the next day they began to throw the cargo overboard. …

When neither sun nor stars appeared for many days and the storm continued raging, we finally gave up all hope of being saved. After the men had gone a long time without food, Paul stood up before them and said: … "Last night an angel of the God whose I am and whom I serve stood beside me and said, 'Do not be afraid, Paul. You must stand trial before Caesar; and God has graciously given you the lives of all who sail with you.' So keep up your courage, men, for I have faith in God that it will happen just as He told me." …

When daylight came, they did not recognize the land, but they saw a bay with a sandy beach, where they decided to run the ship aground if they could. … The soldiers planned to kill the prisoners to prevent any of them from swimming away and escaping. But the centurion wanted to spare Paul's life and kept them from carrying out their plan. He ordered those who could swim to jump overboard first and get to land. The rest were to get there on planks or on pieces of the ship. In this way everyone reached land in safety.

Once safely on shore, we found out that the island was called Malta. The islanders showed us unusual kindness. They built a fire and welcomed us all because it was raining and cold. … They honored us in many ways and when we were ready to sail, they furnished us with the supplies we needed. (Acts 27:1–28:10)

10. How did God rescue Paul and his companions during their journey to Rome? How did God provide for their needs?

11. What word of encouragement did Paul speak to his companions in their anxiety?

12. In what ways does God "open doors" for His people to share the Gospel around the world?

The Catechism

THE CONCLUSION

For Thine is the kingdom and the power and the glory forever and ever.* Amen.

What does this mean? This means that I should be certain that these petitions are pleasing to our Father in heaven, and are heard by Him; for He Himself has commanded us to pray in this way and has promised to hear us. Amen, amen means "yes, yes, it shall be so."
*These words were not in Luther's Small Catechism.

Kingdom. Power. Glory. God gives us His kingdom through Christ. In His power, God rules the universe, the world, and His church through His love in Christ. All glory belongs to God alone, for He has created us, redeemed us in Christ, and sanctifies us through the Holy Spirit.

- God is King, who shares all His good gifts with us!

- God is the almighty Savior, with power to answer our prayers!

- God is Lord, who is worthy of our praise!

13. How would you respond to the question, "Does God really answer our prayers?"

14. In what way is the Lord's Prayer a blessing in your prayer life?

God's People Pray

May the strength of God pilot us.
May the power of God preserve us.
May the wisdom of God instruct us.
May the hand of God protect us.
May the way of God direct us.
May the shield of God defend us.
May the host of God guard us—
against the snares of the evil ones,
against temptations of the world.

May Christ be with us!
May Christ be before us!
May Christ be in us,
Christ be over all!

May Your salvation, Lord,
Always be ours,
This day, O Lord, and evermore.

—St. Patrick

A Verse a Day

Sunday: Consider it pure joy, my brothers, whenever you face trials of many kinds, because you know that the testing of your faith develops perseverance. (James 1:2–3)

Monday: Be self-controlled and alert. Your enemy the devil prowls around like a roaring lion looking for someone to devour. Resist him, standing firm in the faith, because you know that your brothers throughout the world are undergoing the same kind of sufferings. (1 Peter 5:8–9)

Tuesday: Rather, clothe yourselves with the Lord Jesus Christ, and do not think about how to gratify the desires of the sinful nature. (Romans 13:14)

Wednesday: But the Lord is faithful, and He will strengthen and protect you from the evil one. (2 Thessalonians 3:3)

Thursday: The Lord will rescue me from every evil attack and will bring me safely to His heavenly kingdom. To Him be glory for ever and ever. Amen. (2 Timothy 4:18)

Friday: Call upon Me in the day of trouble; I will deliver you, and you will honor Me. (Psalm 50:15)

Saturday: Now to the King eternal, immortal, invisible, the only God, be honor and glory for ever and ever. Amen. (1 Timothy 1:17)

LEADERS NOTES

The format for each session is similar. For notes on how to guide participants through the parts of the Study Guide, see session 1.

As you prepare to lead the session,

- read the Study Guide and answer the questions as fully as possible.

As you prepare for your time together,

- arrive early to make sure the setting is comfortable.
- greet participants by name.
- introduce participants to one another.
- thank participants for their time and commitment.
- keep in mind that sometimes participants may be reluctant to share their thoughts about some issues. Help participants see that God's solid Word guides us as we apply Law and Gospel to our lives. In Christian love we can discuss difficult issues, even though at times we may differ on how God's Word can be applied to our lives.

1 THE MYSTERY OF PRAYER

Pray Together

Use the prayer as you begin the session.

Discover

Read aloud the session theme.

Introduction

Read aloud, or invite a participant to read aloud, the brief introduction to the session. In general, spend 5–10 minutes on the Introduction questions.

- Allow participants to write down and share aloud their questions.
- Answers will vary.
- Answers will vary. Encourage participant discussion.

Read the paragraph "Who?"

God's Word

1. Daniel's accusers represent the various ways people may reject the true God, deny His Word, and pressure His people to compromise or abandon their faith.

2. Daniel believed in God. He entrusted His life to God. He prayed, "giving thanks to God, *just as he had done before.*" The threat of personal harm and deprivation did not shake Daniel's confidence in the grace and power of God.

3. Accept participant responses. God's love and power encourage His people to remain steadfast in faith despite opposition and persecution, to continue to worship God, to pray, to serve others, etc.

Greeting Card

Invite a participant to read the paragraph on greeting cards. Allow participants to reflect on and answer the questions.

- Cover pictures will vary.
- The inside text (words) will vary.

What?

Invite a participant to read the paragraph in this section.

4. Answers will vary. Encourage participant discussion.

5. Answers will vary.

6. Answers will vary.

God's Word

Invite a participant to read aloud this portion from Holy Scriptures. Use the questions for reflection and discussion on the text.

7. St. Paul encourages his fellow Christians to rejoice in the Lord. Believers can know God's peace and be anxiety-free because of Christ's promises. In faith, we can approach God in prayer with every request.

8. Accept participant responses. Believers know God's peace as they pray because they know God will hear their prayers and answer according to His mercy in Christ.

When?

Ask a participant to read the selection from Lloyd John Ogilvie. Use the questions for discussion.

9. God invites us His chosen people in Christ to pray at all times. Ogilvie notes that the "challenges and opportunities" of each day move us to pray, as do the crises we face in life.

10. Answers will vary. If time permits, allow participants to share their responses.

Where?

Invite a participant to read aloud Thomas "Stonewall" Jackson's remarks. Then use the questions for discussion.

11. Answers will vary.

12. Encourage participants to share how corporate prayer has been meaningful in their lives.

13. Allow participants to share their answers and explanations. Though we may be busy, quiet time with God in study of His Word and prayer is the most important use of time.

How?

Invite a participant to read the paragraphs on how to pray.

God's Word

Read aloud, or invite a participant to read aloud this portion of Holy Scripture. Then answer the questions and share your answers together.

14. Jesus teaches His disciples how to pray by giving them a model: The Lord's Prayer. He also demonstrates in His parable that God's people can call on Him in their need; He encourages persistence in prayer; and He gives His promise to answer our prayers according to His goodness and mercy.

15. Allow participants to share their experience with persistence in prayer.

16. Encourage participants to share their comfort in knowing God will answer their prayers.

God's People Pray

Use the prayer as a closing devotion. If you wish, include special prayers for needs of participants, your congregation, your community, the nation or world.

A Verse a Day

Encourage participants to read and memorize the Bible verse for each day. You may want to discuss practical ways to achieve this objective.

2 THE INTRODUCTION AND THE FIRST PETITION

Note: The format for each session is similar. For leader notes on how to guide participants through the parts of the Study Guide, see session 1.

Introduction

- Encourage participants to reflect on the poet's words. It is easy, in one sense, to learn the words of the Lord's Prayer. It takes a lifetime to understand *with the heart* their meaning and application to our lives.
- Answers will vary.
- Allow participants to share their experiences with praying the Lord's Prayer.

The Catechism

Read the selection from Luther's Small Catechism and the following paragraph.

1. Answers will vary. They may include that children enjoy the blessings of shelter, protection, nourishment, teaching, modeling, and support from fathers (and mothers, too!)

2. Answers will vary. Images may include protection, strength, goodness, kindness, gentleness, firmness, help, encouragement, etc. For some individuals, *father* may not carry such positive associations. Allow participants to share their thoughts, feelings, and experiences.

3. God's children may call on Him with "all boldness and confidence" because God has promised to be *our* Father. Most children would never ask another father or person for what they need or want; they

would, rather, ask their own father. Since God is our Father, we can in faith ask often, repeatedly, and boldly, that is, with the assurance God will hear and answer us in His mercy.

God's Word

4. Answers may vary on the characteristics of the father in the parable of the lost son. They may include His patience, understanding, concern, joy over his son's return, patience with his older son, compassion, love, etc.

5. Answers will vary about the sons. They may include recklessness, hostility, disregard for the family, jealousy, hatred, etc.

6. Allow participants to make the connection between the father in the parable and God our heavenly Father.

God our Father

- Jesus began His prayer with *our* rather than *my* because in Jesus all believers are children of the heavenly Father. We pray together as His people—with and for one another.
- Allow participants to share their comfort in knowing all believers pray together "Our Father."

God's Word

7. St. Paul proclaims God as creator of the world, who does not live in temples built by mortal human beings. God is self-existent, that is, does not require anything from His creation for His existence. He gives life to all people. He determines the course of history and nations and peoples. All life has its origin in God, and nothing happens apart from His knowledge or will. We are, by grace, His children through our creation and adopted children by our redemption in Christ.

8. Answers may vary. God's power may appear overwhelming to people when they consider the grandeur of the universe, God's design in creation, and

68

His control over history. God's power is a comfort to His forgiven people in Christ as we consider that He rules over the universe and our lives as a loving Father.

9. God's plan was to save the world through His Son. The "Gospel in a nutshell" summarizes how God accomplished His plan: "For God so loved the world that He gave His one and only Son, that whoever believes in Him shall not perish but have eternal life" (John 3:16). Share additional passages that describe God's plan to redeem all people through Christ.

10. Allow participants to share their blessings through faith in Jesus.

God's Word

11. The Holy Spirit prays for us. The Lord Jesus also prays—intercedes—for us.

12. Allow participants to describe the types of weaknesses we face in life (e.g., anger, addiction, health problems, broken relationships, etc.). Our weaknesses can, in fact, discourage us from praying.

13. When words do not come, we can trust that Christ is still present in our lives, working to draw us closer to Him through His Word, and praying for our faith and endurance.

The Catechism

14. Allow participants to share how God's love and strength have impacted their lives. As time permits, share the various names we use to call on God (Lord, Helper, Savior, Rock, Redeemer, etc.).

15. Worship and Bible study bring us to Christ. True worship is centered on Jesus. The Scriptures center on Jesus, too. As we are connected to His Word, baptized into the saving name of God, and nourished in the Lord's Supper, we grow in faith and service.

3 THE SECOND AND THIRD PETITIONS

Introduction

- Encourage participants to reflect on the word *kingdom* in our day and location.
- Answers will vary.

The Catechism

1. Allow participants to share evidence of God's rule over the universe and human history. Examples may include the consistency and order in the universe, the beauty of creation, and His ongoing protection of humankind.

2. The Lord Jesus rules His church in love, and through His Gospel He calls people to faith, equips and strengthens them for service, and grows His kingdom. Encourage participants to reflect on Christ's rule in their lives and in His church.

3. Accept participant responses. Blessings may include no sickness, pain, hunger, or thirst, a glorified body, reunion with loved ones.

God's Word

4. Sin destroyed the "good and perfect" world God had created for human beings.

5. The serpent was, in fact, the devil. Satan brought sin into the world by tempting Adam and Eve, who yielded of their own free will. Satan, the "old, evil foe," continues to tempt all people today and to work against God's kingdom and purpose in the Gospel.

6. God brought His kingdom of grace into the world through Christ. St. Paul writes, "For he has rescued us

from the dominion of darkness and brought us into the kingdom of the Son he loves, in whom we have redemption, the forgiveness of sins" (Colossians 1:13–14).

The Kingdom of Grace

- The heavenly Father brought us into the kingdom of grace through Baptism, through His Word when we heard and believed the Gospel.
- Allow participants to share their comfort and encouragement as Christ leads them through His Word.

The Catechism

7. Allow participants to share examples of God's activity in our world.

8. Answers will vary. They may include assaults from the world beyond our human ability, pride, substituting our plans and goals for God's purposes, etc.

9. Because Christ is at the heart and center of the Father's plan, we rest content in knowing that what God wills in Christ is our heart's desire.

The Heavenly Father's Will

- Allow participants to share their joy in knowing God wants the best for His people.

God's Word

10. The seed represents the Word of God, the Good News of the Kingdom, at work in different soils, that is, human lives.

11. The soils represent the different attitudes toward God's Word. Some people hear and do not understand; they refuse to believe, or perhaps have no interest in the coming of the Kingdom. In both cases, Satan quickly "snatches away" the good seed. Some people hear and receive the Good News of the kingdom for "a short time." The joy of salvation, however, quickly dissolves, as the fire of "trouble and persecution" burns up the seeds of trust and personal devotion. Still others hear the message,

understand, and believe the Good News, but they soon are overwhelmed by the concerns and snares of everyday life. But in the mystery of God, some hear, understand, believe, and bring forth a crop, a rich harvest of the Spirit's fruit.

12. The parable serves to illustrate God's gracious work among His people through His Gospel. In Christ, God desires the salvation of every person: He wants His kingdom to come and His will to be done in every life. Yet not everyone will hear and believe the Good News.

4 THE FOURTH PETITION

Introduction

- Encourage participants to reflect on the different ways that people—ourselves included—take material blessings for granted.
- Answers will vary. They may include that we soon think and feel that we are responsible for our successes and wealth.

The Catechism

1. Encourage participants to reflect on Luther's explanation of "daily bread" and add any particular needs for our day.

2. God gives His blessings both *immediately* and *mediately*, that is, directly and indirectly, through His appointed means and representatives.

3. Allow participants to share their gratitude for God's "little blessings" in life.

God's Word

4. Answers will vary. They may include "desperate," "hopeless," "extreme," at least, that is, from a human perspective.

5. God provided basic necessities for both Elijah and the widow out of His mercy and His love.

6. The story reveals that God truly cares for His people, and will at times use extraordinary measures to provide for their physical well-being.

Daily Bread

- Allow participants to respond to the statement, "I work hard for everything I have! Why should I be thankful?" As you can, share that God is really the giver of all good gifts—to believers and unbelievers alike. He gives us talents to use to earn a living and manage our resources, but ultimately everything we have comes through His grace.

- Accept participant responses. The gracious Giver's blessings move His people to share with others in need.

This Day

7. Answers will vary. Permit participants to share their needs.

8. Answers will vary. They may include life itself, good health, good news from a neighbor or friend, etc.

9. God gives us the assurance that He will take care of us because of His love in Christ.

God's Word

10. At root, life is a gift from God the creator, and true life centers on God's relationship with us. Our bodies are gifts from God, and God calls us to serve one another in love.

11. Accept participant responses on worry and anxiety.

12. Jesus promises that the heavenly Father will, out of His goodness and mercy, provide what we need along with His greatest gift in the kingdom of God: forgiveness, life, and salvation in Christ.

5 THE FIFTH PETITION

Introduction

- Encourage participants to share their thoughts on the difficulty of forgiving others *in real life*.
- Answers will vary, but will focus on brutality, revenge, hatred, etc. *Hell* is an accurate description.

The Catechism

1. The words that describe our natural, sinful condition are: sins, neither worthy, nor deserving, daily sin much, deserve nothing but punishment.

2. Answers will vary. They may include addictions, suffering, broken relationships, violence, antagonism, etc.

3. God "looks beyond" our sin to see the perfect goodness of Christ. Through faith in Him, we stand before God as forgiven, righteous in His sight.

God's Word

4. Isaiah is terrified: "Woe to me! I am ruined!" The prophet knew that he was a sinner, and that he lived among a sinful people.

5. God, through the seraph, takes away Isaiah's sin and guilt. The "live coal" is a picture of God's means to cleanse His people and bring them forgiveness, that is, through Baptism and the Lord's Supper, His means of grace.

6. Isaiah's response is, "Here I am. Send me on your mission, Lord."

Grace Lake

- Answers will vary. Allow participants to reflect on the imagery of Christ's forgiveness as an "oceanic lake, forgiveness for *any* and all sins."
- Answers will vary. Encourage participants to share how they can bring Christ's love to others.

"As We Forgive Those Who Trespass Against Us"

7. Accept participant responses. Be sensitive to their difficult experiences.

8. Accept participant responses. Again, be sensitive to the diversity of experiences.

9. Encourage participants to focus on the healing power of Christ's forgiveness in their relationships.

Martin Luther's advice is hard to put into practice. Forgiveness has healing power. If we do not forgive, we remain the prisoner. Forgiveness sets *us* free. At times we may have to forgive even though the offender does not ask for forgiveness. Perhaps the offender (because of sinful nature, lack of information, lack of courage, etc.) cannot reach the point of asking forgiveness. Nevertheless, we can forgive because punishment is God's business. ("Vengeance is mine," the Lord says.)

God's Word

10. Joseph's attitude is forgiveness and understanding; he recognizes God's larger purpose and plan in his own suffering.

11. Joseph's attitude again is love, forgiveness, and concern for their future.

12. Joseph provides a picture or "type" of Christ in His rich forgiveness toward sinful, rebellious brothers.

God's Word

13. The wicked servant demonstrates an *unforgiven* and *unforgiving* heart by refusing to forgive his fellow

servant a pittance compared with the amount he himself owed the master.

14. Accept participant responses, but point out that refusal to forgive shows a complete rejection of God's love and forgiveness to us.

15. Encourage participants to share how Christ's limitless love and forgiveness are active in their lives.

6 THE SIXTH AND SEVENTH PETITIONS AND THE CONCLUSION

Introduction

- Encourage participants to share their thoughts on how people view temptation.

- Answers will vary. They may focus on the fact that adolescents and young adults may not realize their own mortality. "No fear" deceives and endangers human life, because we have many reasons to fear in different circumstances.

The Catechism

1. The three enemies that deceive us and lead us toward sin are "the devil, the world, and our sinful flesh."

2. Answers will vary, but may include financial and sexual temptations, abuses of power, apathy, selfishness, etc.

3. God's people overcome temptation and win the victory through Christ, who defeated Satan and redeemed us.

God's Word

4. Answers will vary. They may include the temptation to satisfy our appetites and desires above all else, to test God, to worship something other than the true God.

5. Jesus answers the devil with God's Word. Each time the Lord trusts in God's promise to save and protect His children. As believers, our strength and hope is

found only in God's Word, as Christ speaks His Gospel and makes us stand firm in faith.

6. Accept participant responses.

Leading Us Not into Temptation

- Encourage participants to name the people they turn to for support and encouragement in temptation.
- Answers will vary, but help participants to see their congregation and fellow believers as a valuable source of comfort for all people in need.

The Catechism

7. Answers will vary. They may include violence, lies, drugs, idolatry, immorality, etc. At times, evil can seem to overwhelm people as a storm overwhelms the land.

8. God has rescued us from the greatest evil—Satan, death, and hell—in the gift of His Son, Jesus Christ, for the sins of the world and our sins individually.

9. Accept participant responses on the love and care of God in our daily lives.

God's Word

10. God rescued Paul and his companions by bringing them safely through a tremendous storm. After they landed on the island of Malta, Paul and his fellow travelers were refreshed by the local population.

11. In His mercy, God gave Paul a special message through His angel. Paul could speak confidently to his shipmates because He knew God's purpose for his life: to testify to the Gospel before the Roman emperor. Today God speaks to us in His Word, and He encourages us in our moments of anxiety and despair.

12. Allow participants to explore how God is opening doors around their community and the world to bring the Gospel to all people.

The Catechism

13. Accept participant responses, but focus on the assurance we have in His Word that God does answer our prayers according to His good purpose in Christ.

14. Encourage participants to share how the Lord's Prayer is a blessing in our prayer life.